LinkedIn Profiles That Don't Suck!
Learn the Insider LinkedIn Success Tactics That Will Have Recruiters Calling You!

By The LinkedIn Insider

Teaching Referrals

- Barb & Dave
- Judy
- Sarah
- Ryan & Ideal

Table Of Contents

Do I Need To Be On LinkedIn?

Ability is nothing without opportunity –
Napoleon Bonaparte

Do you need to be on LinkedIn? If you are looking for job or even think you might be looking in the future the answer is an unqualified yes! The simple truth is that the art and process of job hunting has changed radically in just the last two or three years and it's all due to LinkedIn. How do I know? Not only have I worked at LinkedIn as a recruiter in the past I have had the opportunity to talk to many of the top corporate recruiters and headhunters in the industry. I've seen up close what works and what doesn't when it comes to creating terrific LinkedIn profiles. I know that an outstanding LinkedIn profile is as vital to your job search as oxygen is to your health. Here's why.

In any given month over 2.9 million positions are generally filled in the United States of America. However only a fraction of those jobs are ever advertised in any form. The story these recruiters and human resources managers tell me is always the same. Their budgets, never large, have been reduced to almost zero. Advertising for positions costs money that they simply don't have. What's more, even on those rare occasions when they do have the money for advertising they rarely do it for fear of being swamped with resumes. Sorting through job applications takes both time and money, resources these people simply don't have. This is why LinkedIn has become crucial and why it is mandatory that you have a kick ass LinkedIn profile. Average won't cut it.

What I know from experience and from talking with my peers is that a LinkedIn profile now functions like a first interview. When recruiters have a position to fill it allows us to pro-actively search for the top candidates rather than have to react to a tidal wave of unqualified applicants. It allows us to sniff around your profile and find out what people really think of you without having to contact you in the first place. To recruiters and human resources people your LinkedIn profile allows them to evaluate you without you even knowing. If you don't pass this hidden test you'll never get the call and will not even know that you had been considered. The truth is that your LinkedIn profile should be generating 2 or 3 unsolicited calls a week for most professionals. If this is not happening to you then your LinkedIn profile sucks. This is where I can help.

Like I said I have actually worked at LinkedIn as a recruiter, which makes me a double threat. I've seen first hand what works and what doesn't. Through the course of my work I've talked to hundreds of recruiters and job search professionals that have given me a unique perspective. It's really not hard to create a LinkedIn profile that stands out from the crowd if you know what you're doing. This is the information I intend to share with you in this little book.

What I've learned is that, as with so many things in life, the 80/20 rules applies big time with LinkedIn. There are a few big ideas that, if you get them right, will lead you to 80% of your LinkedIn success. It is these big ideas that we are going to explore in this book, as well as some underground tactics that are actually somewhat against official LinkedIn policy (hence my pen name) but that I know work when done correctly. Ready to get started so that amazing job opportunities start to come your way? Turn the page and let's do this, your future awaits.

LinkedIn Success Tactic #1 – Before You Begin

Before anything else, preparation is the key to success
– Alexander Graham Bell

The LinkedIn Insider Says ...

Before we start fixing up your LinkedIn profile it is vital that recruiters are able to find your profile in the first place. Never lose sight of the fact that LinkedIn is really nothing more than a big search engine. When human resource people are looking to fill positions the first thing they will do is perform a search based on a few keywords. You want your profile to appear on the first page of these search results if possible. The deeper your profile appears in the search results the less likely it is that a potential recruiter will find you. This is why your first *"LinkedIn Profiles That Don't Suck!"* action step is to find your top five keywords for your industry.

Action Steps and Notes

1. On the LinkedIn home page type in the job you are looking for in the search box right at the top of the screen. For example, "Web designer".
2. On the left hand side click on "Jobs" to filter the search results so that you only see web designer jobs.

3. Start to click on the results. For any job that looks relevant to you copy and paste the description into a text file. Make sure you include all of the information available, including responsibilities, qualifications, minimum requirement, work experience, education, etc. Do this at least five times.
4. Go to wordle.net.
5. Copy and paste the text file you now have into wordle and run it.
6. Wordle will create a "Word cloud" from the text you have pasted into it. The largest words you see are the words that have been used most often.
7. Write down the top 5 largest and most relevant words that you see. These are your potential keywords. For example, for "Web designer" your keywords might be "web", "designer"," css", "javascript" and "HTML". These are now your keywords.

I've seen some people use job sites like indeed.com when they are searching for job descriptions. However, I have generally gotten better results by working within the LinkedIn ecosystem. The whole point of this exercise is to get the main words that recruiters are likely using when they are searching for potential employees with your skill set. When choosing your keywords always ask yourself, "If I were a recruiter searching for me, would I use this word?" As such when you are picking your top five keywords do not include words that recruiters are not likely to use, such as "Skills".

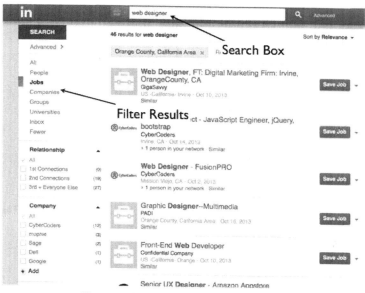

Figure 1: LinkedIn Search Results

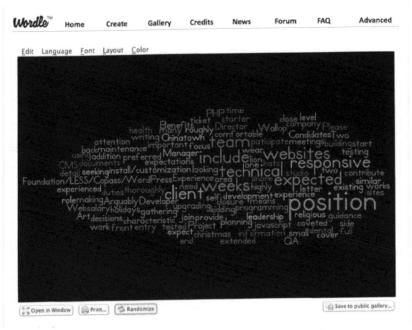

Figure 2: Wordle Search Results

LinkedIn Success Tactic #2 – Get a Professional Photo Taken

A picture is worth a thousand words

The LinkedIn Insider Says ...

After you have nailed down your keywords the next most critical aspect of your profile is your picture. Having a picture is mandatory, full stop. Do a search in LinkedIn for almost any job category and look at the results. Any profile that does not have a picture will typically be ignored. This is a disaster as the whole point of a listing is to get potential recruiters to click through and read your full profile. As well you shouldn't just have any picture on display. Remember that your LinkedIn profile is like a job interview and you want to put your best foot forward at all times. Pay the money and get a professional photographer to take a professional portrait picture of you. Don't have yourself photo shopped or anything like that, but you do want to look your best. Headshots with the eyes looking at the viewer on a plain background work the best. And don't wear brown. No one looks good in brown.

Action Steps and Notes

1. Get a professional photo taken. This is mandatory.
2. The photo should be an accurate representation of you. When you get a face-to-face meeting the interviewer

should not be shocked at how different you look. Your photo should be an honest reflection of you at your best, not a lie. No photo shop.

3. Use a plain, white background if possible. The focus should be on you, not what is in the background.
4. Use the maximum resolution you can.
5. You want to look professional, smiling, and inviting.
6. Don't wear brown.

Figure 3: An Example of a
Professional Photo

LinkedIn Success Tactic #3 – Job Titles and Headline

Try not to become a man of success, but rather try to become a man of value – Albert Einstein

<u>The LinkedIn Insider Says ...</u>

Once you have your professional picture in hand the next thing you need to refine is your job title(s) and headline. I always recommend using three suitable job titles if possible. An example of this would be "Social Media Instructor", "Social Media Trainer" and "Social Media Consultant". Why three job titles? Once again remember that LinkedIn is a search tool for potential employers and the more job titles you have, the more likely you are to be found. This is also the first opportunity you have to use your keywords if appropriate.

The next tactic is the really big one though. Although many savvy LinkedIn profiles use multiple job titles, very few use an attention-grabbing headline that offers a benefit. Remember that recruiters are looking for people who can help them fill a position. If you were a recruiter looking for a Google advertising expert and these two profiles came up, which one would you click on first?

Profile A

Bob Roberts
Google AdSense certified | Media Consultant

Profile B

Pam Garst
Google AdSense certified | Social Media
Trainer | Ask me how I increased the ad
revenue for my last employer by 500%!

Can you see the difference? By having a benefit statement listed right in her professional headline Pam is making it clear that she understands what potential employers are looking for and that she has a record of success. You need to make your profile stand out to get that click and this is what Pam does. This is what you need to do too.

Action Steps and Notes

1. Use three job titles in your professional headline and make use of your keywords if appropriate.
2. Add a short line that includes a benefit statement. Make it clear that you have something to offer to your potential employer.

LinkedIn Success Tactic #4 – Make It Easy to Connect

Always bear in mind that your own resolution to succeed is more
important than any other – Abraham Lincoln

The LinkedIn Insider Says ...

To this day I find it amazing how many profiles there are on LinkedIn with no contact information whatsoever. No phone number, no e-mail address, nothing. Recruiters have told me time and time again how frustrating this is for them. When we are looking to fill a position we are typically on a tight deadline and competing with other recruiters as well. We don't have time to Google you and we rarely want to pay for LinkedIn in-mail. Ideally we want a phone number to call. If you don't want to give out your phone number I suggest you use Google voice. The next best option is an e-mail address, but a phone number is always preferred. You need to get real. If you want to get hired you need to be easily accessible to recruiters and potential employers.

Action Steps and Notes

I strongly suggest you provide as much contact information as you can and that you make use of all of the items below if possible.
1. Provide a phone number. If you do not wish to do this use Google Voice.

a. http://www.youtube.com/watch?v=cOZU7BOeQ58 - See this YouTube video for a great 1 minute description of Google Voice

b. https://www.google.com/voice

2. Provide an e-mail address. If you do not want to provide your own set up a Hotmail or Gmail account.

3. Include blogs or twitter accounts that are professional in nature.

4. If you don't have a webpage (or even if you do) I suggest you set up a page at about.me. This service makes it easy to set up an attractive page filled with contact information that you can use in LinkedIn.

a. https://about.me/

5. Change your LinkedIn public profile link. This is the link that LinkedIn automatically generates and by default it usually looks like http://www.linkedin.com/pub/brett-mcdonald/a/rr5/234. It is very easy to change this to something like www.linkedin.com/in/brettmcdonald (by clicking on "Edit" in your profile), which is much more pleasing to the eye.

LinkedIn Success Tactic #5 – The Background Section

Strive not to be a success, but rather to be of value – Albert Einstein

The LinkedIn Insider Says ...

Once again this section, if you do it right, should be all about making it easy for people to contact you and explaining what you can do for them. At the very top of the summary I suggest you place your phone number as this should appear "above the fold" (meaning it will be visible as soon as someone navigates to your page) and you can never make it too easy for potential employers to contact you. Next have a section listing the ways you can help your future employer. Always remember that you are selling yourself and what you can do. Make it clear whom you can help, how you do it and who you are. One guerrilla tactic that I do recommend you do is at the bottom to have a section entitled "Here is how you can help me" or "These are the opportunities I am interested in". The idea here is that if a recruiter reads this and can't use you he may well know someone who can! Successful recruiters network like crazy and we help each other out when possible. Don't miss out on this step!

Action Steps and Notes

1. Place your phone number right at the top so that it is easy to see.
2. Sell yourself by explaining what you can do for your potential employer.
3. At the bottom don't forget to outline the other opportunities you might be interested in.

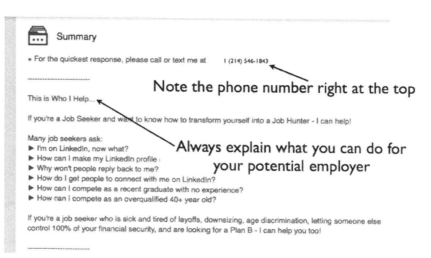

▣ Summary

* For the quickest response, please call or text me at   1 (214) 546-1843

This is Who I Help...

If you're a Job Seeker and want to know how to transform yourself into a Job Hunter - I can help!

Many job seekers ask:
► I'm on LinkedIn, now what?
► How can I make my LinkedIn profile
► Why won't people reply back to me?
► How do I get people to connect with me on LinkedIn?
► How can I compete as a recent graduate with no experience?
► How can I compete as an overqualified 40+ year old?

If you're a job seeker who is sick and tired of layoffs, downsizing, age discrimination, letting someone else control 100% of your financial security, and are looking for a Plan B - I can help you too!

Note the phone number right at the top

Always explain what you can do for your potential employer

Figure 4: An Example of a Great Summary Section

LinkedIn Success Tactic #6 – The Experience Section

Experience: that most brutal of teachers. But you learn, my God do you learn – C.S. Lewis

The LinkedIn Insider Says ...

You may have noticed that I have skipped the "Skills and Expertise" section and gone right to the "Experience" part. The reason for this is that I have never talked with a recruiter or human resources person who has taken the "Skills and Expertise" section seriously (I know I didn't). LinkedIn has made it far too easy for anyone to just randomly click and endorse you for a skill, whether they really believe you have that skill or not. This makes this section almost worthless. If you want to get hired you need to focus on the "Experience" section. This is where the action is.

When writing about your previous experience recruiters don't want to read long, windy stories about your life. Use short, concise paragraphs with numbers whenever possible. By numbers I mean statements like "I helped 150 people to 200 each week" or "I increased sales by 25% over my term". The reason why you want to use numbers is that they appear to be more factual and less arbitrary. Don't get me wrong; I'm not saying to make numbers up. Just use relevant truthful facts whenever possible.

This final point is the most important by far though. You need to get quality recommendations from people you have worked with in the past whenever possible. Quality recommendations are the exact opposite to the "Skills and Expertise" section for recruiters. Recommendations take time to write and recruiters know that the people who write them stand behind them, they just haven't clicked on a link. How do you get recommendations? The easiest way I have seen is to simply start giving them out. Whenever you give out a recommendation LinkedIn will prompt the recipient to recommend you back. If you have given them a nice recommendation they will typically return the favor. Most recruiters, in a perfect world, are looking for recommendations from a boss, a peer, and someone who has worked under you. This gives them a well-rounded perspective on just who you are and what you are bringing to the table. From what I've seen giving out two recommendations a day works best as you don't want to get a flood of recommendations back on the same day, as it will look kind of fishy. Once you have 10 you are good to go for most recruiters, although there is nothing wrong with more.

Action Steps and Notes

1. Don't concern yourself overly with the "Skills and Expertise" section. Most recruiters and human resources people simply skip over it.

2. Use short, concise paragraphs to describe your previous work experience. Use relevant, truthful numbers to back up what you are saying whenever possible.
3. Aim to get at least 10 quality recommendations from people whom you have worked with. To get recommendations, give them out.

Figure 5: Recruiters Rarely Look at this Section

LinkedIn Success Tactic #7 – Education and the Rest

Always bear in mind that your own resolution to succeed is more important than any other –
Abraham Lincoln

The LinkedIn Insider Says ...

As with the other sections a potential employer is going to use this section to try and fill in the blanks about you to get a complete picture. Be sure to include any extracurricular activities you may have been involved in. Potential employers are attracted to well-rounded individuals, not just people who went to school and then schlepped their way home. In most cases I wouldn't include your high school unless you are very young or went to a very prestigious institution.

One suggestion I do have for this section is to create what I call a "Keyword dumping ground". Remember that LinkedIn is a search engine so the more keywords you can get in here the better. As an example let's say you are in the technology field. I would create a school and name it "Skills/Technology". Below this "school" I would place all of the keywords that an employer might be looking for such as "IP Telephony", "Cisco Routers", "Lan, Wan, San" etc. Making up "schools" like this and listing your knowledge below them is a great way to get found in LinkedIn.

Action Steps and Notes

1. To show that you are a well-rounded individual be sure to include any extracurricular activities you were involved in.
2. Don't include your high school unless it is prestigious or you are very young.
3. Create headings as "schools" in order to keyword dump the skills you have that potential employers might be looking for.

Boston University
General Liberal Arts & Sciences
1989 – 1991

Activities and Societies: American Red Cross Instructor, Emergency Medical Technician, EMT, Emergency Medical Services, EMS, Hockey

Saint Francis Preparatory High School
1985 – 1989

Activities and Societies: Concert Band, Jazz Band, Marching Band, Judo, Karate, Volunteer Ambulance

Skills / Technology

Project Management (Utilized)
- PMI / PMP / PgMP
- PMLC, SDLC
- Six Sigma, DMAIC, DMADV
- ITIL (Service Transition)
- Process Re-Engineering
- ISO 9000
- MISMO

Technology
- ATM, SONET, Metro Ethernet, T1 / T3
- Audio / Video (AV) Conferencing
- BlackBerry Enterprise Server
- Call Center, ACD, PBX
- Cisco
- DSL, Frame Relay, ISDN

Not a school but allows you to list searchable words

Figure 6: The Education Section

Guerilla Tactic #1 – Billboard Recommendations

Definiteness of purpose is the starting point of all achievement
—W. Clement Stone

The LinkedIn Insider Says ...

This is a sneaky tactic that I've seen work wonders. Never lose sight of the fact that the whole point of LinkedIn is to get noticed by potential employers. Let's say you could put up a giant billboard saying "Hire ME!" right at a busy intersection where you know that potential employers for your skills always stop. Wouldn't this be effective? You can do the same thing in LinkedIn in a couple of ways. Here's how.

The first way is to get in contact with someone you know who is considered to be a "Thought Leader" in your industry. Former bosses work great, but it can also be someone you met at an industry conference. What you want to do is connect with them and then create a thoughtful and well-written recommendation for them. When recruiters are looking for good people they frequently start at the top. They will start with your thought leader's profile when low and behold they will see your recommendation. This elevates you in their eyes and there is an exceptionally good chance they'll click on your profile as well.

The second way is to connect with someone you haven't actually met. Let's say you want to be hired as a social media guru. You find someone who has written a book and is known as a social media guru. For this example let's say it's Seth Godin. Send a request to connect with Seth and tell him that you loved his book and want to give him a glowing recommendation. Seth will likely accept your request and your name will now be on his page. It is literally like setting up a billboard advertising your services on the busiest street in town.

Action Steps and Notes

1. Connect with thought leaders in your industry and give them recommendations. These will act like advertising billboards that will lead directly to you. I've seen it work time and time again.

Guerilla Tactic #2 – Supersize Your Network

Don't wait. The time will never be just right. – Napoleon Hill

<u>The LinkedIn Insider Says ...</u>

This is one tactic that few people do and frankly it amazes me. The name of the game on LinkedIn is to have as many connections as possible. A person with 20 million connections is much more likely to be found than one with 10 thousand. Numbers matter. What this means is that you need to make connections with people who already have large personal networks. On LinkedIn these people are known as LIONS (LinkedIn Open Networks).

When someone identifies himself or herself as a LION (they will typically mention this somewhere in their profile) they are saying they are willing to connect with anyone. If you send them a request to connect they will accept it, no questions asked. Of course you will be better off if you connect with LIONS who are in your industry.

The easiest way to find quality LIONS is to go to a website called TopLinked.com. TopLinked is a website filled with open networkers, including LIONS. This is not a suggestion this is mandatory. Go to this website NOW and sign up for it. I've known people who have gone from 0 to 10 million connections overnight. Why most people don't use this website is beyond me. Don't be one of them. Make use of it now.

Action Steps and Notes

1. Go to TopLinked.com and start supersizing your network now.

Guerilla Tactic #3 – The Ultimate Strategy

I am not a product of my circumstances. I am a product of my decisions. –Stephen Covey

<u>The LinkedIn Insider Says ...</u>

This last strategy is one that I KNOW LinkedIn hates (I did work there, after all) but it works like a charm. The key thing here is to use that ancient form of communication known as the phone and actually talk to people. In today's world I truly feel that the art of talking is a lost art. People just don't do it anymore. They'll tweet, text or e-mail but very few people will actually take the initiative and talk to another person. When you overcome this mental hurdle and actually talk to people doors will open for you. In essence you will be doing what real life recruiters do. By doing the following you will become a recruiter for yourself. This is a very powerful strategy.

The first step is to figure out which 10 to 20 companies you want to work for. It does not matter if the firms you wish to work for are hiring at the moment or not. You want to be on their radar screen so that they never even post the job. This is step one.

Next you will then use LinkedIn or the Internet to figure out who runs the departments in which you wish to be employed. Who actually runs and makes the hiring decisions? Here's the trick though. You will not actually call this person once you have them identified (at least not right away). This is what everyone tries to do and from what I've seen it rarely works. Here's what you will do instead.

Again using LinkedIn, you will find people who used to work for these companies and with your targeted individuals simply call them up and say, "Hey Tim, this is [your name], we're connected on LinkedIn". By mentioning that you are connected on LinkedIn all of the resistance you might normally encounter will just melt away. You're not some stranger making a cold call, you're part of his or her LinkedIn family. Next you ask, "I'm interested in your former employer. Do you have 5 minutes to answer some questions about them?" As this person no longer works there they will likely be completely open to answering your questions. If they say no ask them when it would be convenient for you to call them back.

From there you will talk to this person to gather information about your target company. If you do this well there is a good chance the person you are contacting will communicate with your potential employer and say, "Wow, I just talked to [your name] and he has some great ideas to help your firm. You might want to talk with him". If the person with whom you are talking doesn't contact their former employer you will have at least some valuable information on your target. When you do contact your future employer you will be able to make it clear that you know their issues and how you can help them. There isn't an employer in the world that will not be impressed by this.

Action Steps and Notes

1. Identify which companies you want to work for and how you can add value if they hire you.
2. Identify who runs the departments in the companies you want to work for.
   a. You should be able to get this information by going to the companies website or by doing a search on LinkedIn.
   b. If the above doesn't work you can call the company and ask "Who runs X department?"
3. Identify people who used to work with your targets (company and person). You want to get information about the person you are targeting, their department and the company in general. All of these questions will help you prepare for a potential future job interview. Below are some ideas on what you might want to ask.
   a. Questions about your potential boss
      i. Did you work directly for person X?
      ii. What is he/she like to work for?
      iii. What does potential boss look for in potential employees?

    iv. Can this person make hiring decisions?

    v. What is this person's temperament like?

    vi. Would you say that potential boss looks out for the people under him or her?

    vii. What would you say is potential bosses biggest accomplishment?

    viii. What goals has potential boss set for himself or herself?

b. Questions about your potential future department

    i. How competitive is the department within the industry?

    ii. Is it growing or shrinking?

    iii. Is this department respected within the company?

    iv. Does the rest of the company view this department as a revenue generator or a cost center?

    v. How is this department doing relative to the rest of the company?

    vi. What are the challenges facing this department in the future?

c. Questions about the company

    i. How is the company doing financially?

ii. What does this company do well vs. its competitors? What does it need to work on?

iii. What is this company's growth strategy?

iv. Who are this company's best customers?

v. What are the new customers this company would like to acquire?

vi. Does this company treat its employees well? What is the turnover like?

vii. Can you think of anyone else I should talk to?

viii. Would you work there again if you could?

ix. Why did you leave?

1. This is important to know because if the person has a beef with the company it will likely affect all of their answers and needs to be taken into account.

d. The last question you MUST ask.

i. If I decide to talk with them, can I say I spoke with you?

1. If the person is positive about their former company using their name will likely help you in the future.

2. This may prompt this person to contact their former employer in some way to talk about you and how great you are. This is a VERY good thing!

e. Now that you have done your research it is time to contact your future employer. Again I suggest you use the phone and name-drop the previous employees you've talked to. Make it clear you understand their issues and have ideas on how to solve them. Do this and you'll be ahead of 99.99% of your competition.

FAQ

*Go confidently in the direction of your dreams. Live the life you have imagine –
Henry David Thoreau*

I want to make X change to my LinkedIn profile but I'm not sure how to do it and the LinkedIn HELP isn't very helpful.

I've always found the LinkedIn help to be a bit of a mess with document links not working or being hopelessly out of date. I suggest that you always use Google when you want to look something up for LinkedIn. Google will either direct you to the right page in LinkedIn or list other sites that will help you.

How exactly do most recruiters use LinkedIn?

Most recruiters cast a very wide net and then start adding keywords to narrow their search results down. They'll start with a term like "Project manager", and then they'll add a city, then specific skill sets. Their whole goal is to whittle down 50,000 search results down to 50. That is why having a properly structured LinkedIn profile with a large network is so important. You must appear in that group of 50, preferably near the top, or you won't get the call. And just to be clear having a large network does matter when search results are returned. A person with 12 million connections has a distinct advantage over someone with 12.

You recommended giving out recommendations to get them. Isn't this kind of artificial? Also, wouldn't a recruiter notice that person A and B have recommendations for each other and see it as being kind of phony?

Not in the least. This is the way that LinkedIn works. People expect you to be giving and receiving recommendations. Another factor is that all of the recruiters I have talked to are extremely busy. They don't have time to click on your recommendations to see if they are reciprocal in most cases anyway. Recommendations are extremely important to have and you need to get them, end of story.

Do I need to have a personal website?

Having a personal website is not mandatory, but it is something you might want to build towards in the future. In lieu of a personal website, I do recommend you set up a page using About Me (https://about.me/). It is very easy to set up a simple website using this service and you can fill it with contact information.

I'm not on Twitter or Facebook. Does this lessen me in the eyes of potential employers?

Not in the least. In fact if you are looking for a job and you're spending time on Twitter and Facebook you likely are not looking hard enough. It's not that important.

How can I connect with Super Connectors (people with large networks) on LinkedIn?

The best way is to join groups that contain super connectors. Once you are in the same group send the super connector a connection request. Don't forget to tell them why you want to connect!

LinkedIn Glossary

Believe you can and you're halfway there. –
Theodore Roosevelt

Channel: These are curated topics that can be subscribed to if they are of interest. Some examples might be channels related to technology or marketing.

Company Page: Company pages are just like profile pages but companies use them. They typically display information related to job openings, services offered and general news.

Connections: These are the people that you have made a connection with on LinkedIn. You can connect with other LinkedIn users through 3 degrees of separation. 1st degree connections are those people you are directly connected with. 2nd degree connections are uses that are connected to you by your 1st degree connections. 3rd degree connections are people you are connected with through your 2nd degree connections.

Groups: Groups are collections of LinkedIn users with common interests based on industry, topic, or association. You can join groups or create your own.

IDKU: Usually seen on profiles as "I will never IDKU" which translates as "I will never tell Google I do not know you". You never want to be marked as an IDKU as you could be marked as a spammer, which might result in you being kicked out of LinkedIn.

Influencer: A LinkedIn user who provides information that can be subscribed too.

Influencer Feed: This feed displays updates from the channels and influencers you are following.

InMail: This is LinkedIn's internal mail system. However it can only be used by premium members or purchased by a member.

Introductions: This feature allows you to request an introduction to a person via one of your own connections.

Invitation: These are requests you can send to connect with other users.

OpenLink Network: This is a service only offered to premium members. OpenLink members can contact all other OpenLink members without the need of having a previous connection.

Out of Network: LinkedIn members with whom you are not connected with in anyway.

Profile: This acts as your resume within LinkedIn and should list all of your career information.

Recommendations: There are references that other members can post about you as well as you can post about other members. These are very important to have as they allow others to vouch for your abilities and skills.

Settings: Allows you to control what you and others see in LinkedIn related to your profile.

Update Feed: Similar to a Facebook feed this page displays all of your network's activity.

Your Network: Your entire group of connections, including members of any groups you may belong to.

Resources

The best way to predict the future is to invent it – Alan Kay

Below are some links to various apps and websites that you might find helpful. The links are up-to-date as of this writing but be aware that LinkedIn has a history of changing them at a moments notice. If the links I've provided below don't work simply do a search in Google and you will be able to find them.

Resume Builder

Resume builder allows you to transform your profile into a resume quickly and easily. LinkedIn will also create a webpage for your resume, which makes it easy to share across any social networks you may have.

http://resume.linkedinlabs.com/

LinkedIn App for Mobile

LinkedIn has created a great mobile app for IOS, Android, Blackberry and Windows. It allows you to access all of the features that are available on the website and it's a great help when you need to recall contact information when you are away from the office.

LinkedIn for iPhone and iPad

https://itunes.apple.com/us/app/linkedin/id2 88429040?mt=8

LinkedIn for Android

https://play.google.com/store/apps/details?id
=com.linkedin.android&hl=en

LinkedIn for Blackberry

http://appworld.blackberry.com/webstore/con
tent/7605/?countrycode=US&lang=en

LinkedIn for Windows

http://www.windowsphone.com/en-
us/store/app/linkedin/bdc7ae24-9051-474c-
a89a-2b18f58d1317

LinkedIn University

LinkedIn continues to create content in the
form of training videos and manuals in order
to help users become proficient on their
platform. It is always worth checking out.

LinkedIn University

http://university.linkedin.com/index.html

About the Author

The LinkedIn Insider (not his real name) worked for over three years as a recruiter at LinkedIn. In that time he learned first hand the simple things that need to be done to make a profile successful. This is his first and most likely will be his only book on the subject.

One Last Thing

When you turn the page Kindle will give you the opportunity to rate the book and share your thoughts through an automatic feed to your Facebook and Twitter accounts. If you believe your friends would get something valuable out of this book, I'd be honored if you'd post your thoughts. As well, if you liked the book, I'd be eternally grateful if you posted a review on Amazon. Thank-you once again and I sincerely hope my book has put you on the road to getting the job you desire.

15135258R00033

Made in the USA
San Bernardino, CA
15 September 2014